PLANT EXPERIMENTS
What Affects Plant Growth?

Mary Ann Hoffman

REAL LIFE readers™

Rosen Classroom™

New York

Published in 2009 by The Rosen Publishing Group, Inc.
29 East 21st Street, New York, NY 10010

Book Design: Daniel Hosek

Photo Credits: Cover (foreground) © Pakhnyushcha/Shutterstock; cover (background) © Orientaly/ Shutterstock; pp. 3, 4, 6, 8, 10, 12, 14, 16, 18, 20, 22, 23, 24 © 2happy/Shutterstock; p. 5 (top) © Andy Z./Shutterstock; p. 5 (inset) © Eduardo Rivero/Shutterstock; p. 7 (flower) © Photodisc; p. 7 (roots) © Brandon Blinkenberg/Shutterstock; p. 11 © Kevin R. L. Hanson/DK Stock/Getty Images; p. 13 © PM Images/ Photographer's Choice/Getty Images; p. 15 © Nicholas Piccillo/Shutterstock; p. 17 © Marc Dietrich/ Shutterstock; p. 19 (top) © Daniel Hosek; p. 19 (bottom) © Denis Miraniuk/Shutterstock; p. 21 © Linda MacPherson/Shutterstock; p. 22 © MPI/Hulton Archive/Getty Images.

Library of Congress Cataloging-in-Publication Data

Hoffman, Mary Ann, 1947-
    Plant experiments : what affects plant growth? / Mary Ann Hoffman.
        p. cm. — (Real life readers)
    Includes index.
    ISBN: 978-1-4358-0131-8
    6-pack ISBN: 978-1-4358-0132-5
    ISBN 978-1-4358-2971-8 (library binding)
    1. Growth (Plants)—Juvenile literature. 2. Plants—Experiments—Juvenile literature. I. Title. II. Series.
    QK731.H594 2009
    571.8'2--dc22

                                         2008036786

Manufactured in the United States of America

CONTENTS

PLANTS: PARTS AND FUNCTIONS

Plants are an important part of Earth's **ecosystems**. They've **adapted** to grow in many different **environments**— dry, wet, hot, and cold.

Do you know some things that make a plant different from an animal? Most plants make their own food from air, sunlight, and water. Animals can't do that. Plants can't move from place to place under their own power. Animals are able to move around. People and other animals depend on plants for food and goods they need in order to live.

Look at these rain forest and desert plants. Do you know some of the ways they've adapted to their environments?

Most plants have four basic parts that animals don't have. These parts are leaf, stem, flower, and root. The roots hold the plant in place and draw water and **nutrients** from the soil. The stem holds the plant up and moves water and nutrients from the roots to the other parts. The leaf makes food for the plant. The flower makes **pollen** and seeds that help create new plants.

Have you ever looked at plants in a garden or field and wondered why they grow the way they do? In this book, you'll find some fun experiments that may help you answer some of your questions.

flower — makes pollen and seeds to create new plants

leaf — makes food for the plant

stem — holds the plant up and moves water and nutrients from the roots to other parts

root — holds the plant in place and draws water and nutrients from the soil

WHAT IS AN EXPERIMENT?

An experiment is a way to find an answer to a question by testing to see what happens. The plant experiments in this book follow the **scientific method**—an ordered way of conducting an experiment that includes asking questions, constructing a **hypothesis**, experimenting, observing and recording **data**, drawing conclusions, and reporting results.

The scientific method is a tool scientists use to help them guess a possible outcome, think about what might cause it, and test possible solutions. It's a system that looks for cause and effect.

The Scientific Method

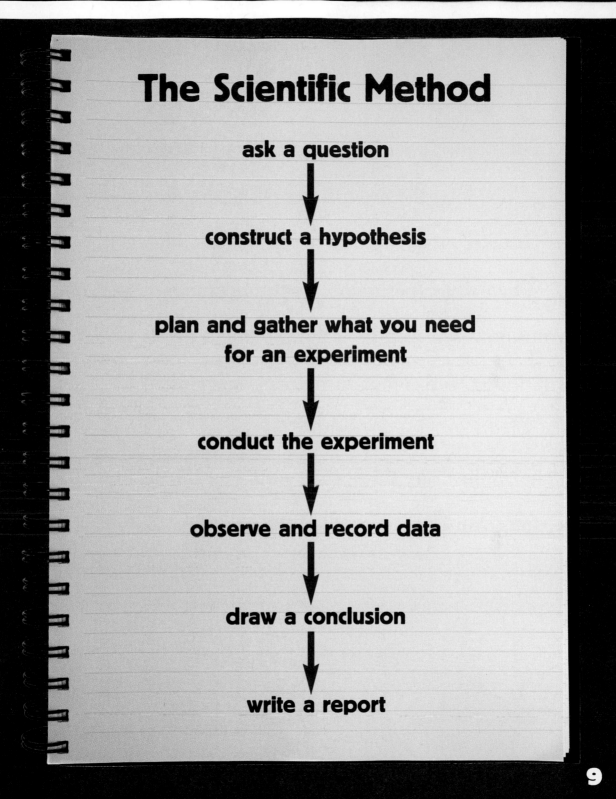

ask a question

construct a hypothesis

plan and gather what you need
for an experiment

conduct the experiment

observe and record data

draw a conclusion

write a report

The scientific method requires controlled conditions such as how long the experiment takes, the **materials** needed, where it takes place, and the order of steps followed.

When you experiment, it's important to have controls so you know why you get the results you do. If you change many things each time you redo an experiment, you won't know what caused your results. So, in an experiment, you can change just one thing each time you do the experiment. The thing you change is called the variable.

Some experiments require safety glasses like the ones worn by the teacher and student on page 11.

SUNLIGHT AND PLANT GROWTH

Most plants need sunlight to grow. In this experiment, we will see how sunlight **affects** plants.

Question: How does sunlight affect plant growth?

Materials:
- 2 plastic cups or small pots
- 2 small green plants
- soil
- water
- window or table in the sunlight
- cardboard box

Method:
1. Place equal amounts of soil into each pot.
2. Put one plant into the soil in each pot.
3. Place the pots near the window or on a table in the sunlight.
4. Place a cardboard box over one of the pots.
5. Lightly water each plant every day for 2 weeks—be careful to put the box back over the same plant after each watering.

Observation: After 2 weeks, the plant in the uncovered pot is green and has grown. The plant that was covered is no longer as green and has died.

Conclusion: Plants need sunlight to stay green and grow.

Which of these plants was in the sunlight?

WATER AND PLANT GROWTH

You just read an experiment that showed the effect of sunlight on plant growth. What do you think would happen to plants that don't get water? Try the next experiment to find out!

Question: How does water affect plant growth?

Materials:
- 2 plastic cups or small pots
- soil
- grass seeds
- water
- window or table in the sunlight

Method:
1. Place equal amounts of soil into each pot.
2. Sprinkle grass seeds into each pot and press them lightly into the soil.
3. Place the pots near the window or on the table in the sunlight.
4. Put tape or a mark on one pot.
5. For 2 weeks, lightly water only the marked pot.

Observation: After 2 weeks, grass is growing in the pot you watered. Grass didn't grow in the pot that wasn't watered.

Conclusion: Plants need water to grow.

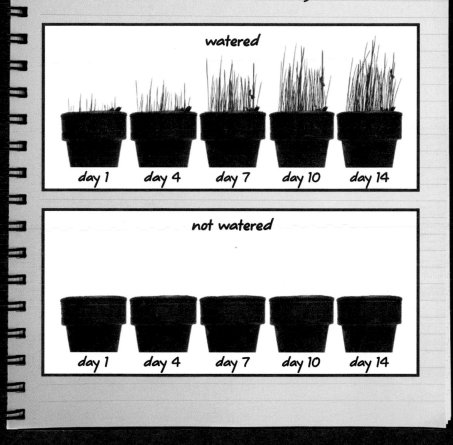

This experiment shows that without water, the grass didn't grow. What do you think would happen to seeds planted in a garden if it didn't rain and they weren't watered?

WHAT HAPPENS WHEN PLANTS GET LESS AIR?

You've read two experiments that showed what happens to plants that don't get sunlight or water. What do you think would happen to plants if they didn't get enough air? Try the following experiment to find out!

Question: What happens when plants get less air?

Materials:
- two small potted plants with several leaves on each plant
- **petroleum jelly**
- window or table in the sunlight
- water
- notebook

Method:

1. Mark one pot with tape.
2. Take the plant in the marked pot and cover the bottom side of its leaves with petroleum jelly.
3. Place the two plants in the sunlight.
4. Lightly water both plants every day.
5. In the notebook, make a drawing of the plants every day for 2 weeks.

Observation: The plant with the coated leaves became weak and less green.

Conclusion: The petroleum jelly prevented the leaves from getting enough air and making enough food for the plant. Plants that get less air aren't healthy.

Do you think this plant's leaves are getting enough air and making food? Why or why not?

HOW DOES WATER TRAVEL TO A PLANT'S FLOWER?

Plants get water from the ground through their roots. Did you ever wonder how water gets from a plant's roots to the leaves or flowers at the top of the plant?

Question: How does water travel to a plant's flower?

Materials:
- clear glass jar
- water
- blue food coloring
- spoon
- white flowers with stems

Method:
1. Pour water into the jar.
2. Put several drops of blue food coloring into the water and stir with the spoon.
3. Place the flowers into the colored water.
4. Watch the flowers for about 3 days.

Observation: The flowers have turned blue.

Conclusion: The flowers turned blue because the blue-colored water traveled up the plant's stem.

What color do you think these flowers will be in a few days? Why do you think that?

DO PLANTS KNOW WHICH WAY IS UP?

Bean plants grow from bean seeds. When a bean seed is planted in the ground, the roots grow down into the soil and the stem grows up out of the soil. Do plants know which way is up? Here's an experiment that shows how roots and stems grow.

Question: Do bean seed roots and stems know which way to grow?

Materials:
- bean seeds
- clear plastic zip bag
- paper towels
- water
- tape
- window
- notebook

Method:
1. Soak paper towels in water.
2. Fold the wet towels and lay them flat in the plastic bag.
3. Place a few bean seeds on the towels and seal the bag so the seeds are flat against the plastic.

Method (continued):

4. Tape the bag to a sunny window.
5. After the seeds **sprout**, make a drawing of the seeds every day.
6. After a few days, turn the bag upside down and tape it to the window again.
7. Continue to make a drawing of the new plants each day.

Observation: When the seeds sprouted, the roots grew down and the stems grew up. After the bag was turned upside down, the roots bent to keep growing down and the stems bent to keep growing up.

Conclusion: Roots of bean seeds grow down and their stems grow up. Plants sense that their roots need water that's down in the ground and their stem needs sunlight that's up above the ground.

This picture shows how the roots and stem of a bean seed grow.

YOU'RE THE SCIENTIST!

In this book, you've read some simple plant experiments and learned about things that affect how plants grow.

You can try these experiments yourself and compare your observations and conclusions with those you've read about.

You may have other questions about how plants grow, too. Plan your own experiments and use the scientific method to record and share your results, just like scientists do!

George Washington Carver was a scientist who completed many plant experiments.

GLOSSARY

adapt (uh-DAPT) To change to fit new conditions.

affect (uh-FEHKT) To act on something and cause a change.

data (DAY-tuh) Facts gained from an experiment.

ecosystem (EE-koh-sihs-tuhm) A group of living and nonliving things and the place where they live.

environment (ihn-VY-ruhn-muhnt) Everything that surrounds a living thing.

hypothesis (hy-PAH-thuh-suhs) An educated guess.

material (muh-TIHR-ee-uhl) A tool or thing needed for an experiment.

nutrient (NOO-tree-uhnt) Something needed to live and grow.

petroleum jelly (puh-TROH-lee-uhm JEH-lee) A soft, oily jelly with many different uses.

pollen (PAH-luhn) A fine yellow dust found in some flowers.

scientific method (SY-uhn-tih-fihk MEH-thud) An ordered system used to complete an experiment.

sprout (SPROWT) To begin to grow.

INDEX

A
air, 4, 16, 17

C
conclusion(s), 8, 9, 13, 15, 17, 19, 21, 22
controlled conditions, 10
controls, 10

D
data, 8, 9

F
flower(s), 6, 7, 18, 19
food, 4, 6, 7, 17

H
hypothesis, 8, 9

L
leaf(ves), 6, 7, 16, 17, 18

N
nutrients, 6, 7

O
observations(s), 13, 15, 17, 19, 21, 22
observe(ing), 8, 9

P
pollen, 6, 7

Q
question(s), 6, 8, 9, 12, 14, 16, 18, 20, 22

R
report(ing), 8, 9
results, 8, 10, 22
root(s), 6, 7, 18, 20, 21

S
scientific method, 8, 9, 10, 22
seeds, 6, 7, 14, 20, 21
soil, 6, 7, 12, 14, 20
stem(s), 6, 7, 18, 19, 20, 21
sunlight, 4, 12, 13, 14, 16, 17, 21

V
variable, 10

W
water, 4, 6, 7, 12, 14, 15, 16, 17, 18, 19, 20, 21

Due to the changing nature of Internet links, The Rosen Publishing Group, Inc., has developed an online list of Web sites related to the subject of this book. This site is updated regularly. Please use this link to access the list: http://www.rcbmlinks.com/rlr/plexp